UNITED STATES MILITARY MEDALS AND DECORATIONS

by Jack Britton

Art Work
Glen McBeath

ISBN 0-912958-03-0

Printed in the United States of America

M.C.N. Press (Military Collectors' News Press)

P.O. Box 7582 Tulsa, Oklahoma 74105

The first decoration was created by Congress in 1780 for the capture of a British Intelligence Officer, Major John Andre, and since that time many medals and decorations have been struck for award for Heroism, Service, Campaigns, ect.

This book was printed only as a guide for collectors' and historians' and is complete as we could make it, we used line drawings rather than photos, so we could show more detail (all medals are not drawn to scale).

We hope that this book will be of help to you, in identifing U.S. medals.

1. Presidential Medal of Freedom

Awarded for: Contributions towards national security and interest, world peace and culture.

Ribbon: Blue bordered in white

Notes: It is worn as either a breast or neck decoration.

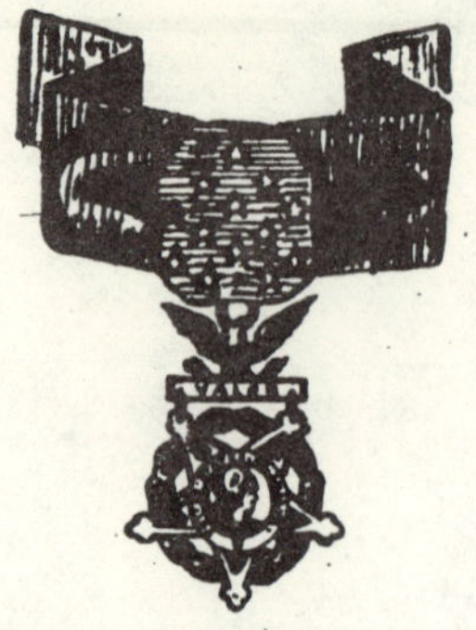

2. Medal of Honor (Army) 1904 to present

Awarded for: Valor (the nation's highest award)

Ribbon: Blue and a pad of blue ribbon with thirteen stars.

3. Medal of Honor (Army) 1904 to ?

The same medal as number 2, but with a pin-back ribbon.

4. Medal of Honor (Army) 1862–1896

Awarded for: Valor

Ribbon: Top third is blue with vertical red and white stripes below.

5. Medal of Honor (Army) 1896–1904

Same as the 1862–1896 version, except the ribbon was changed to vertical red center stripe flanked by blue and red at each edge.

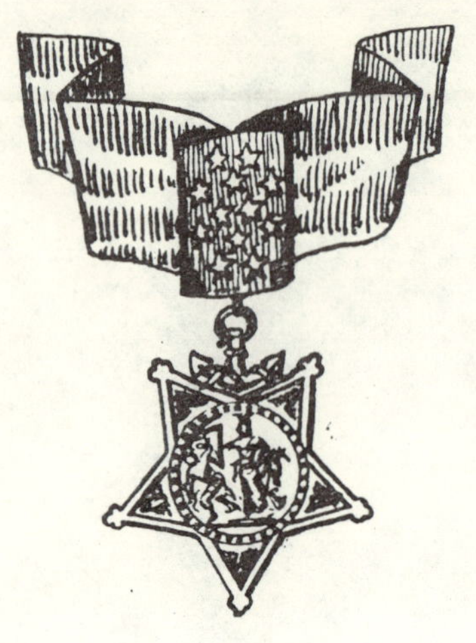

6. Medal of Honor (Navy) 1942 to present

Awarded for: Conspicuous gallantry and intrepidity at the risk of life, above and beyond the call of duty, in action involving actual conflict with an opposing armed force.

Ribbon: Blue and a pad of blue with thirteen stars.

7. Medal of Honor (Navy) 1917–1942

Awarded for: Same as number 6.

Ribbon: Blue with thirteen stars, pinback.

8. Medal of Honor (Navy) 1913–1919

Awarded for: Conspicuous gallantry and intepidity at the risk of life, above and beyond the call of duty, in action involving actual conflict with an opposing armed force.

Ribbon: Blue with thirteen stars.

9. Medal of honor (Navy) 1862–1913

Same as above, but with a change to the ribbon.

Ribbon: **Top** third is blue with vertical red and white stripes below.

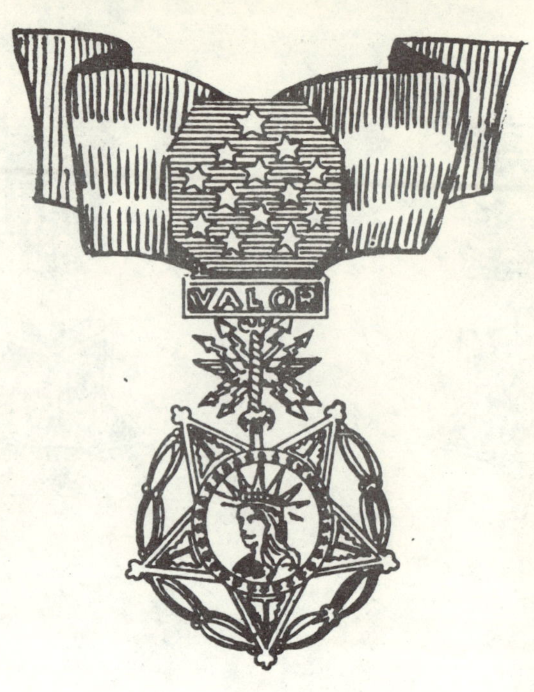

10. Medal of Honor (Air Force)

Awarded for: Conspicuous gallantry and intepidity at the risk of life, above and beyoun the call of duty, in action involving actual conflict with an opposing armed force.

Ribbon: Blue and a pad of blue with thirteen stars.

Notes: The ribbon bar worn on the uniform is the same for all services.

11. Navy Cross

Awarded for: Extraordinary heroism in connection with military operations against an opposing armed force.

Ribbon: Navy blue with a white center stripe.

Notes: The navy's second highest award.

12. Air Force Cross

Awarded for: Extraordinary heroism in connection with military operations against an opposing armed force.

Ribbon: Light blue edged with white and red stripes.

Notes: The Air Force second highest award.

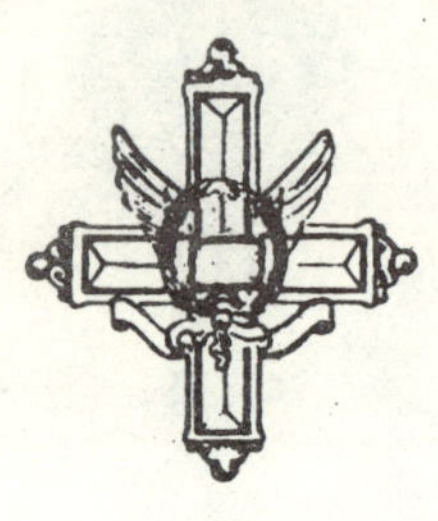

13. Distinguished Service Cross (Army)

Awarded for: Extraordinary heroism in connection with military operations against an opposing armed force.

Ribbon: Dark blue , narrow white stripe and red on edges.

Notes: The Army's second highest decoration.

14. Distinguished Service Cross (Army) 1st Style

Awarded for: Same as above.

Ribbon: Same as number 13.

Notes: Less than 100 of these were awarded

15. Distinguished Service Medal (Air Force)

Awarded for: Exceptionally meritorious service to the Government in a duty of great responsibility.

Ribbon: Center of white flanked by gold stripe and wide blue, and edged in gold.

16. Distinguished Service Medal (Navy)

Awarded for: Exceptionally meritorious service to the Goverment in a duty of great responsibility.

Ribbon: Navy blue with center stripe gold.

17. Distinguished Service Medal (Navy) 1st style

Awarded for: Exceptionally meritorious service to the Government in a duty of great responsibility.

Ribbon: Navy blue with center stripe of gold, same as 2nd style.

18. Distinguished Service Medal (Army)

Awarded for: Exceptionally meritorious service to the Government in a duty of great responsibility.

Ribbon: Center of white flanked each side by blue, edged in red.

19. Distinguished Service Medal (Merchant Marine)

Awarded for: Exceptionally meritorious service to the Government in a duty of great responsibility.

Ribbon: Red center flanked by stripes of white and dark blue edges.

20. Distinguished Service Medal (Coast Guard)

Awarded for: Exceptionally meritorious service to the government in a duty of great responsibility.

Ribbon: Blue center flanked by thin white stripe with purple on either edge.

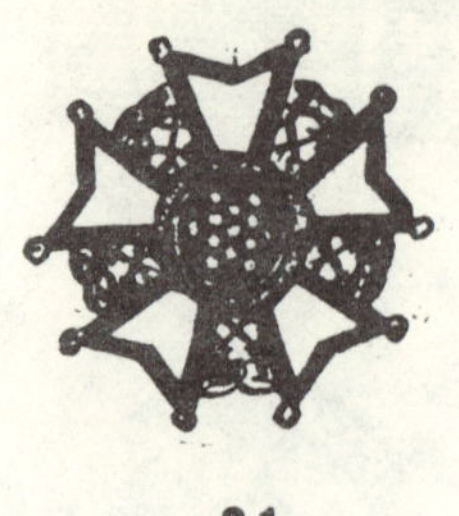

21

22

23

24

21. Legion of Merit (Chief Commander) Heads of Governments.
22. Legion of Merit (Commander) Equivalent of a Chief of Staff.
23. Legion of Merit (Officer) Generals and flag rank.
24. Legion of Merit (Legionnaire) All others eligible.

Awarded for: Exceptionally meritorious conduct in the performance of outstanding service.

Ribbon: Purplish red with thin stripe of white on each edge.

25. Coast Guard Medal

Awarded for: Acts of heroism not involving conflict with an opposing armed force.

Ribbon: Center and edges blue, eight white stripes and six red stripes.

26. Soldiers Medal

Awarded for: Acts of heroism not involving conflict with an opposing armed force.

Ribbon: Two outside stripes of blue and a center of seven white and six red stripes of equal width.

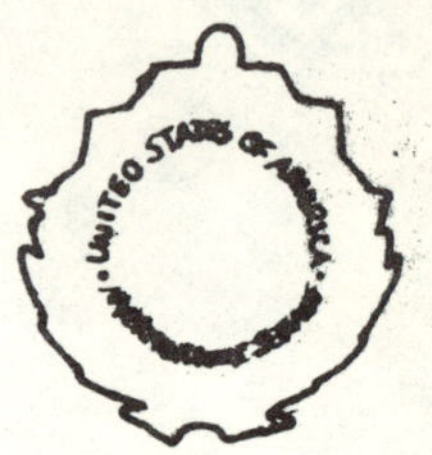

27. Airman's Medal

Awarded for: Acts of heroism not involving conflict with an opposing armed force.

Ribbon: Edges of light blue and alternateing in the center 13 stripes of yellow and dark blue.

28. Meritorious Service Medal

Awarded for: Outstanding non-combat meritorious achievement or service to the United States.

29. Distinguished Flying Cross

Awarded for: Heroism or extraordinary achievement while participating in aerial flight.

Ribbon: Blue with narrow stripe of red bordered by white in center and near each edge a stripe of white.

30 Air Medal

Awarded for: Meritorious achievement while participating in aerial flight.

Ribbon: Blue with orange stripe near each edge.

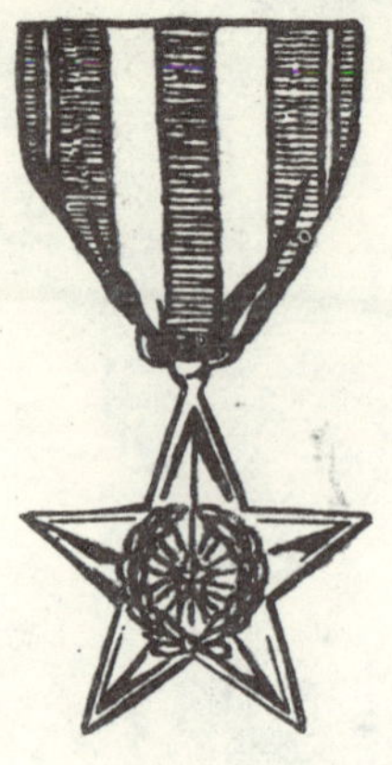

31. Silver Star

Awarded for: Gallantry in action against an opposing armed force.

Ribbon: Red center, flanked on each side by white, blue, white, and blue.

32. Bronze Star

Awarded for: Heroic or meritorious achievement or service, not involving aerial flight, in connection with operations against an opposing armed force.

Ribbon: Red, with blue center, flanked on each side by thin white stripe, edges thin white stripe.

33. Purple Heart

Awarded for: Wounds or death as result of an act of any opposing armed force.

Ribbon: Purple with thin white edges.

34. Badge of Military Merit

Awarded for: Meritorious Service.

Notes: Sometimes this badge had the word "Merit" embroidered on it, this badge was hand made, so many variations may be seen.

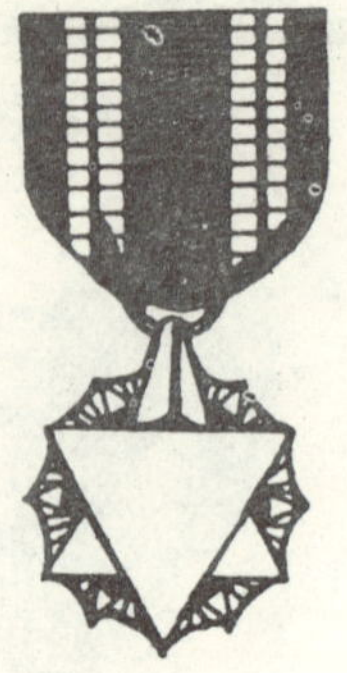

35. Combat Readiness Medal (Air Force)

Awarded for: Completion of an aggregate of four years of sub-tained professional service as an Air Force combat-ready aircrew member.

Ribbon: Wide red center flanked by wide stripes of light blue with thin stripes of dark blue in center, red on either edge.

36. Joint Service Commendation Medal

Awarded for: Outstanding performance of duty or meritorious achievement while assigned to a Joint Staff or or Joint Activity of the Department of Defense.

Ribbon: Green center, on either side are stripes of white, green and again white, and edges of light blue.

37. Gold Lifesaving Medal

Awarded for: Heroic deeds in saving life from perils of the sea. Awarded through the Coast Guard.

Ribbon Wide gold center flanked on each side by thin stripe of white and red stripe at either edge.

38. Silver Lifesaving Medal

Awarded for: Deeds, lessor in degree than that of the Gold Lifesaving Medal, in saving life from perils of the sea. Awarded through the Coast Guard.

Ribbon: Wide silver center flanked on each side by thin stripe of white and blue stripe at either edge.

Notes: Both of the above medals come in two sizes, the earlier ones were larger.

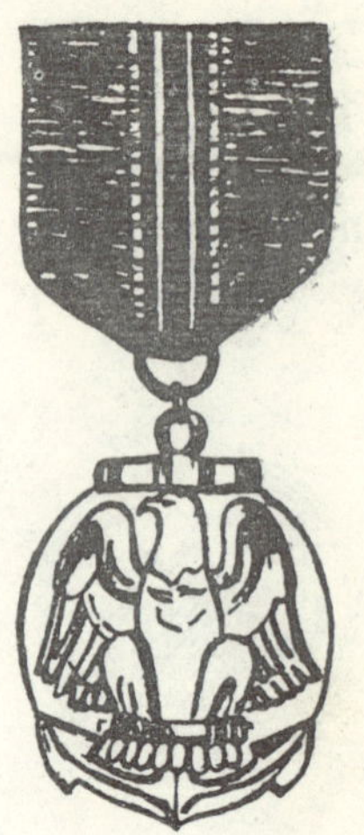

39. Brevet Medal (Marine Corps)

Awarded for: Members of the Marine Corps who held a brevet commission for bravery in action.

Ribbon: Dark red with 13 white stars.

40. Merchant Marine Meritorious Service Medal

Awarded for: Meritorious conduct, commended by the Administrator of the War Shipping Administration.

Ribbon: Blue, center dark blue flanked by white, red, and yellow.

41. **Medal for Merit**

Awarded for: Civilians of nations waging war under a joint declaration with the U.S.

Ribbon: Magenta with two white stripes.

Notes: This medal was awarded to the super spy chief William Stephenson (A man called INTREPID.)

42. Certificate of Merit

Awarded for: Merit and courage, was originally a certificate awarded to enlistmen only, authorized Jan. 1905.

Ribbon: White center stripe with red, white and blue on either side.

43. Specially Meritorious Service Medal

Awarded for: The officers and enlisted men who aided in the attemp to block the Santiago Harbor July 1898.

Ribbon: Bright scarlet

44. Coast Guard Commendation Medal

Awarded for: Meritorious service resulting in unusual and outstanding achievement.

Ribbon: Green with thin white stripe in center and two wide stripes of white near each edge.

45. Navy Commendation Medal

Awarded for: Both Navy and Marine Corps for meritorious or heroic achievement or service.

Ribbon: Green with two wide stripes of white near each edge.

46. Air Force Commendation Medal

Awarded for: Meritorious achievement or service.

Ribbon: Yellow with wide and two thin stripes of blue in center and blue edges.

47. Army Commendation

Awarded for: Meritorious achievement or service.

Ribbon: Green with five thin stripes in center and white on either edge.

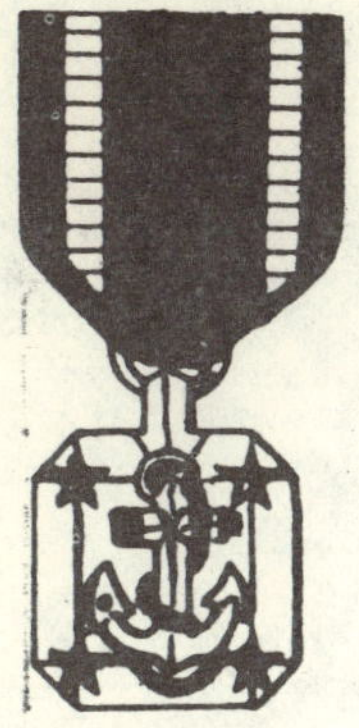

48. Navy Achievement Medal

Awarded for: Junior officers and enlisted men whose professional achievements exceed normal expectancy. For both Navy and Marine Corps.

Ribbon: Green with two wide stripes of orange near edge.

49. Navy and Marine Corps Medal

Awarded for: Acts of heroism not involving actual conflict with an opposing armed force.

Ribbon: From left to right, blue, gold, red.

50. **Medal of Freedom**

Awarded for: Any foreign citizen who aids the U.S. after December 7, 1941 against an enemy.

Ribbon: Red with four thin white stripes near the center.

Notes: This medal is awarded in four degrees, and is awarded to U.S. citizens in lowest degree only.

51. China Service Medal (Navy)
52. China Service Medal (Marine Corps)

Awarded for: Service in china between 7 July 1937 and 7 September 1939 and again between 2 September 1945 and 1 April 1957 for operations in Taiwan and the Matsu Straits.

Ribbon: Yellow with two red stripes near each edge.

Notes: Navy or M.C. is spelled out on reverse.

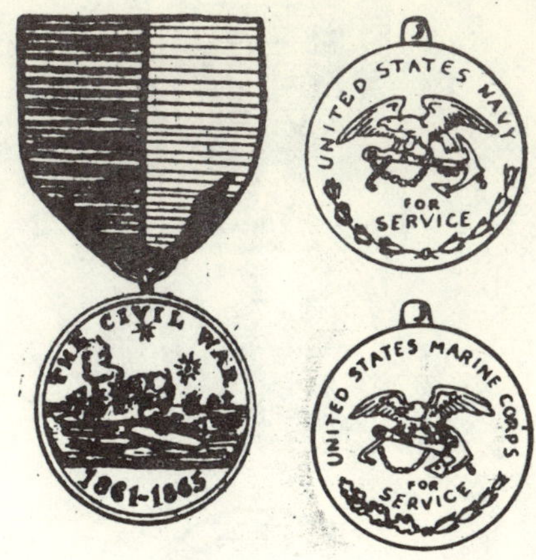

53. Civil War Medal (Army)

Awarded for: Service in the Union Forces between April 15, 1861 and April 9, 1865. And to August 20, 1866 for service in Texas

Ribbon: Left to right, blue and gray.

54. Civil War Medal (Navy)
55. Civil War Medal (Marine Corps)

Awarded for: Service in the Union Forces between April 15, 1861 and April 9, 1865.

Ribbon: Left to right, blue and gray. Same as Army.

56. Cuban Pacification Medal (Army)

Awarded for: Service in Cuba between October 6, 1906 and April 1, 1909.

Ribbon: Olive-drab center flanked on each side by blue, white, and red on edges.

57. Cuban Pacification Medal (Navy)
58. Cuban Pacification Medal (Marine Corps)

Awarded for: Service ashore and on some ships between September 12, 1906 and April 1, 1909.

Ribbon: Olive-drab center flanked on each side by blue, white, and red on edges, same as Army.

Notes: Navy and M.C. same except reverse has Navy or Marine Corps spelled out.

59. Nicaraguan Campaign Medal (Navy)
60. Nicaraguan Campaign Medal (Marine Corps)

Awarded for: Service ashore or on some ships between August 28, 1912 and November 2, 1912.

Ribbon: Dark red with wide blue stripe near each edge.

Notes: Above two are alike, except Navy or Marine Corps is spelled out on reverse.

61. Second Nicaraguan Campaign Medal (Navy)
62. Second Nicaraguan Campaign Medal (Marine Corps)

Awarded for: Service in Nicaragua between August 27, 1926 and January 2, 1933

Ribbon: Red with eight thin white stripes.

Notes: Navy or Marine Corps is spelled out on reverse. This medal was awarded to a few U.S. Army members who participated in the campaign.

63. Yangtze Service Medal (Navy)
64. Yangtze Service Medal (Marine Corps)

Awarded for: Service ashore or aboard certain ships between September 3, 1926 and October 21, 1927, also between March 1, 1930 and December 31, 1932.

Ribbon: Blue with red and yellow stripes near each edge.

Notes: Both the above same except for reverse.

65. Haitian Campaign Medal 1915 (Navy)
66. Haitian Campaign Medal 1915 (Marine Corps)

Awarded for: service in Haiti between 9 July 1915 and 6 December 1915 aboard certain ships or ashore.

Ribbon: Dark blue with two red stripes in center.

Notes: Both above medals are same except for reverse.

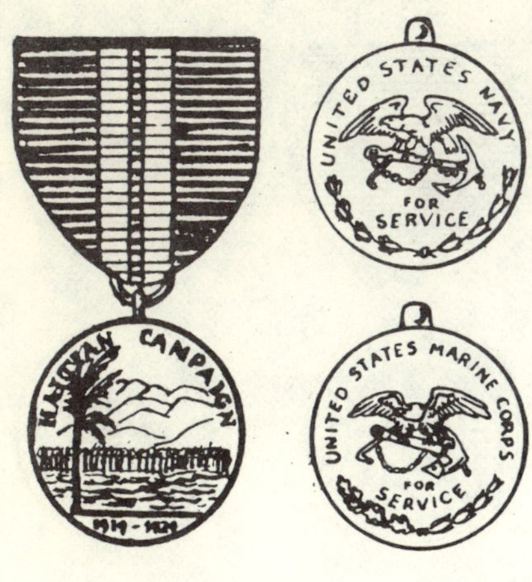

67. Haitian Campaign Medal 1919–1920 (Navy)
68. Haitian Campaign Medal 1919–1920 (Marines Corps)

Awarded for: Service in Haiti ashore or aboard ships between April 1, 1919 and June 15, 1920.

Ribbon: Blue with two stripes of red in center, same as the one for the 1915 medal.

69. Philippine Congressional Medal

Awarded for: Service past discharge date and were ashore in the Philippine Island between 4 February 1899 and 4 July 1902, and were in the service between 21 April 1898 and 26 October 1898.

Ribbon: Dark blue flanked each side by white, red, white, and again dark blue on edges.

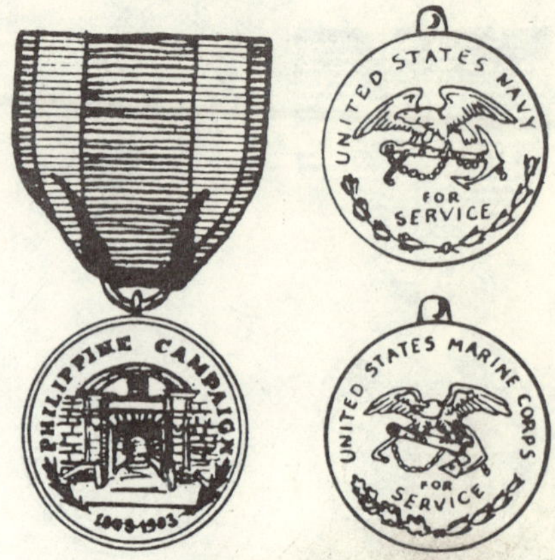

70. Philippine Campaign Medal (Army)

Awarded for: Service in the Philippine Islands from 4 February 1899 and 31 December 1913

Ribbon: Blue with two red stripes near each edge.

71. Philippine Campaign Medal (Navy)
72. Philippine Campaign Medal (Marine Corps)

Awarded for: Service on ships or ashore in the Philippine Island between 4 February 1899 and 4 July 1902.

Ribbon: Blue with two red stripes near each edge. Same as the one for the Army.

73. Mexican Service Medal (Army)

Awarded for: Service in Mexico or Texas between April 12, 1911 and February 7, 1917

Ribbon: Blue center flanked each side by yellow, green stripe on each edge.

74. Mexican Service Medal (Navy)
75. Mexican Service Medal (Marine Corps)

Awarded for: Service in Mexico or Texas, between April 12, 1911 and February 7, 1917.

Ribbon: Blue center flanked each side by yellow, green stripe on each edge, same as one for Army.

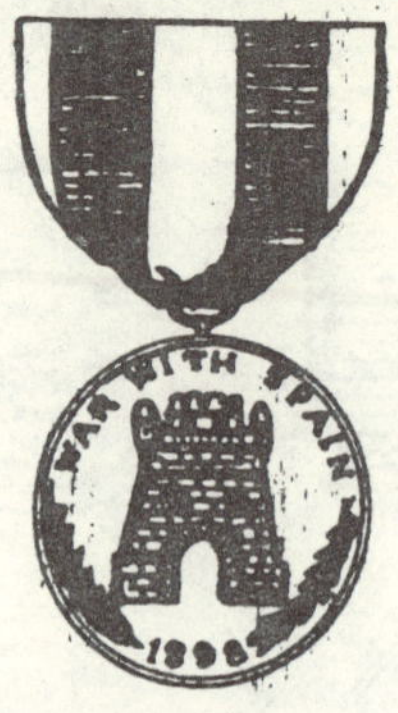

76. Spanish Campaign Medal (Army)

Awarded for: Service in Cuba from 11 May 1898 to 17 July 1898; in Puerto Rico from 24 July 1898 and August 13, 1898; and in the Philippine Islands from 30 June 1898 to 13 August 1898.

Ribbon: Yellow with two wide stripes of blue.

77. Spanish Campaign Medal (Navy)
78. Spanish Campaign Medal (Marine Corps)

Awarded for: Service on ships or ashore in Cuba, Puerto Rico, Guam or the Philippines from April 20, 1898 to December 10 1898.

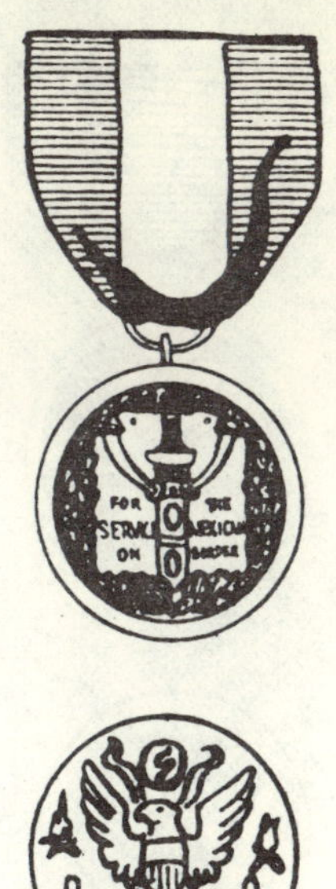

79. Indian Campaign Medal (Army)

Awarded for: The campaigns against hostile American Indians between 1865 and 1898 a span of 32 years, it was not authorized until January 1905.

Ribbon: Red with two black stripes near edges.

80. Mexican Border Service Medal (Army)

Awarded for: Service on the Mexican border between 9, May 1916 and 24, March 1917 for National Guard members, and 1, January 1916 and 6, April 1917 for Army members.

Ribbon: Green with wide yellow center stripe.

81. Spanish War Service Medal (Army)

Awarded for: Service between April 20, 1898 and April 11, 1899 but not eligible for the Spanish Campaign Medal.

Ribbon: Green with two wide yellow stripes.

82. China Campaign Medal (Army)

Awarded for: Service ashore in China between June 20, 1900 and May 27, 1901 (Boxer Rebellion).

Ribbon: Yellow with dark blue edges

83. China Relief Expedition Medal (Navy)
84. China Relief Expedition Medal (Marine Corps)

Awarded for: Service ashore with the Feking Relief Expedition between May 24, 1900 and May 27, 1901, also to personnel on some ships in Chinese waters.

Ribbon: Yellow with dark blue edges.

85. Army of Puerto Rico Occupation Medal

Awarded for: Service in Puerto Rico between August 14, 1898 and December 10, 1898.

Ribbon: Wide blue stripe in center, flanked by thin yellow, and wide red stripes and edges of blue.

86. Army of Cuba Occupation Medal

Awarded for: Service in Cuba 18, July 1898 to 20, May 1902.

Ribbon: Blue center, flanked by thin yellow, wide red, and thin blue on edges.

87. West Indies Naval Campaign Medal, 1898

Awarded for: Participation in the West Indies operations from 27, April to 14, August 1898.

Ribbon: Red with blue center.

Notes: This medal is sometimes called the "Sampson Medal", it is awared to both the Navy and Marine Corps.

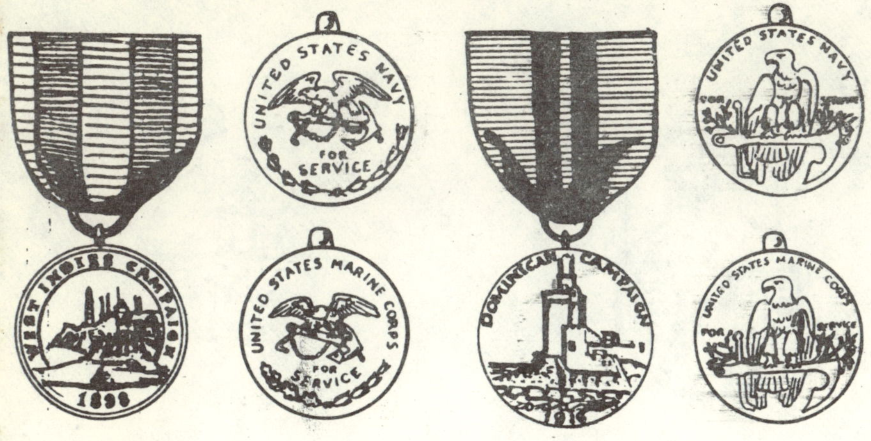

88. West Indies Campaign Medal (Navy)
89. West Indies Campaign Medal (Marine Corps)

Awarded for: Service aboard ships in the West Indies.

Ribbon: Yellow with two wide stripes of blue.

90. Dominican Campaign Medal (Navy)
91. Dominican Campaign Medal (Marine Corps)

Awarded for: Service in the Dominican Republic or on specific ships from 5 May 1916 and 4 December 1916.

Ribbon: Red with two stripes of blue in center.

92. Dewey Medal or Manila Bay Medal

Awarded for: The men who took part in the Battle of Manila Bay, and served on one of the following ships: USS Olympia, USS McCulloch, USS Concord, USS Baltimore, USS Boston, USS Petrel and the USS Raleigh.

Ribbon: Gold center and navy blue on each edge.

93. Korean Service Medal

Awarded for: Service in the Korean area between 27 June 1950 and 27 July 1954.

Ribbon: Light blue with white center and edges.

94. Womens Army Corps Service Medal

Awarded for: Service in both the Women's Army Auxillary Corps and the Women's Army Corps during World War II.

Ribbon: Green with gold edges.

95. Mariner's Medal

Awarded for: Hazardous exposure, wounds or injury from actions by enemy forces.

Ribbon: From left to right, Red, white, and blue.

96. Humane Action Medal (Berlin Airlift)

Awarded for: 120 days service in or with U.S. Armed Forces supplying Berlin Germany, from 26 June 1948 to 30 September 1949.

Ribbon: Thin center stripe of red, flanked each side by thin white stripe, wide blue, thin white and wide black stripes on edges.

97. United Nations Service Medal

Awarded for: Service in the Korean area in support of U.N. action from 27 July 1950 to 27 July 1954.

Ribbon: Blue with white stripes.

98. United Nations Medal

Awarded for: Personnel for not less than six months' service with one of the following United Nations' units: U.N. Observers Group in Lebanon; U.N. Truce Supervision Organization in Palestine; U.N. Military Observers Group in India and Pakistan.

Ribbon: Blue with two white stripes.

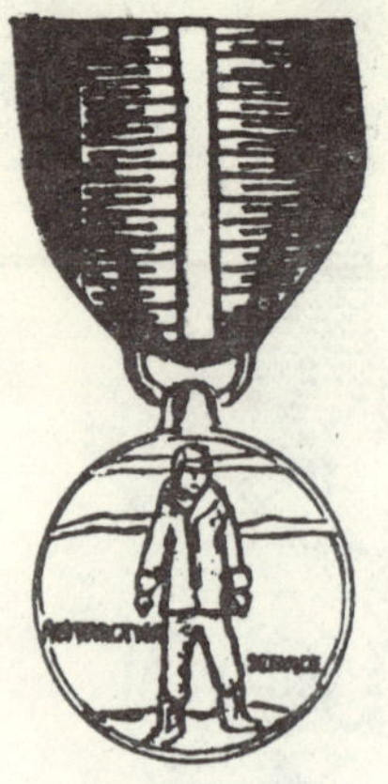

99. Antarctica Service Medal

Awarded for: Participating in an expedition, operation, or support of a U.S. operation in Antarctica.

Ribbon: White center flanked by darker and darker shades of blue, black edges.

100. Republic of Vietnam Campaign Medal.

Awarded for: Service in Vietnam for a period of six months after July 1960, the medal is awarded by the government of South Vietnam, it is authorized by the Department of Defense.

Notes: This medal is manufactored in both the U.S. and Vietnam. (until the pull-out of U.S. troops.)

101. Navy Expeditionary Medal

Awarded for: Opposed landing on foreign territory, such as the Cold War of 1954–65 when Navy personnel landed in the Congo.

Ribbon: Blue edges and center with two yellow stripes.

102. Marine Corps Expeditionary Medal

Awarded for: Opposed landing on foreign territory, authorized March 1929, but awarded for the 1903 expedition to Abyssinia.

Ribbon: Red edges and center with two gold stripes.

103. Vietnam Service Medal

Awarded for: Service in Vietnam and contiguous waters from 1, July 1958 to date unknown.

Ribbon: Yellow, edged in green with three thin stripes of red in center.

104. Victory Medal

Awarded for: Service of thirty days from 7, December 1941 to 3, September 1945.

Ribbon: Red center flanked by stripes of white, blue, green, and yellow, wide red stripes on either edge.

105. Vietnam Service Medal

Awarded for: One years service for civilian employees of the U.S. Government in Vietnam.

Ribbon: Blue, with three stripes of gold, red, and gold in center and near each edge.

106. Armed Forces Expeditionary Medal

Awarded for: Participating in designated expeditions after 1, July 1958.

Ribbon: From left to right, green, yellow, brown, black, wide stripe light blue, dark blue, white, red, again wide stripe light blue, black, brown, yellow, green.

107. Asiatic–Pacific Campaign Medal
Awarded for: Service in the Asiatic– Facific Theater WW II.

Ribbon: Orange, white, red and blue.

108. European–African–Middle Eastern Campaign Medal
Awarded for: Service in the EAME Theater, WW II.

Ribbon: Brown, green, white, red, black and blue.

109. American Campaign
Awarded for: Service in the American Theater, WW II

Ribbon: Four stripes of blue, in center are three stripes blue, white, and red, and near each side are stripes of white, red, black, white.

110. American Defence Service Medal

Awarded for: Service during national emergency, 8 September 1939 to 7 December 1941.

Ribbon: Yellow with thin stripes of red, white and blue, (the blue is to the outside).

111. Occupation of Germany Medal WW I (All Services')

Awarded for: Service in Germany or Austria–Hungary from 12 November 1918 to 11 July 1923.

Ribbon: Black with blue, red and white on either edge.

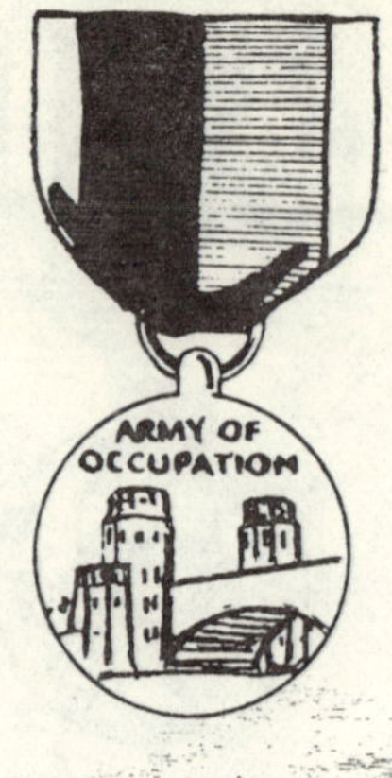

112. Occupation Medal, WWII (Army)

Awarded for: 30 consecutive days' service after WW II at a normal post of duty while assigned to an army of occupation.

Ribbon: Two wide stripes of black and red and white on each edge.

113. Occupation Medal, WW II (Navy)
114. Occupation Medal, WW II (Marine Corps)

Awarded for: Same as Army.

Ribbon: Same as Army.

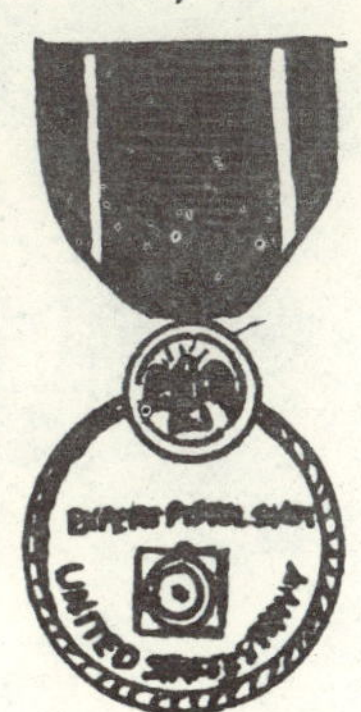
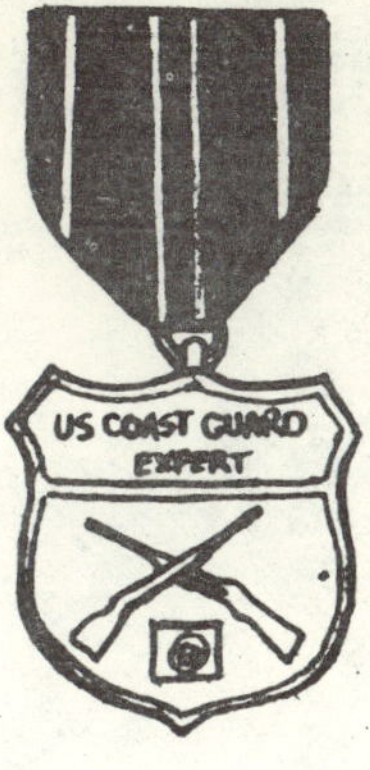

115. Expert Rifle Shot (Navy)
116. Expert Pistol Shot (Navy)
117. Expert Rifle Shot (Coast Guard)
118. Expert Pistol Shot (Coast Guard)

Awarded for: Rigidly prescribed marksmanship requirements.

Ribbons: Navy: Green stripes. Coast Guard: White stripes.

119. Good Conduct (Coast Guard

Awarded for: Four years of continuous service, exemplary behavior, efficiency and fidelity.

Ribbon: White center stripe and maroon at edges.

120. Good Conduct (Navy) 1884 to present

Awarded for: Four years of continuous service, exemplary behavior, efficiency and fidelity.

Ribbon: Dark Magenta.

Notes: Both the Navy and Coast Guard Good Conduct service time has been changed to 3 years.

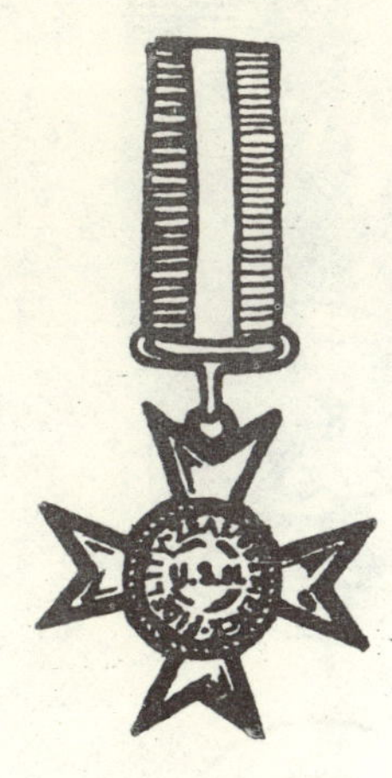

121. Good Conduct (Navy) 1869–1884

Awarded for: Obedience, sobriety, and cleanliness and held a Continuous Service Certificate (given after 3 years service.

Ribbon: From left to right, red, white, and blue.

122. Good Conduct (Army)

Awarded for: Exemplary behavior, efficiency, and fidelity.

Ribbon: Red with three white stripes at each edge.

123. Good Conduct (Air Force)

Awarded for: Same as above

Ribbon: Blue with three stripes of red, white and blue at each edge.

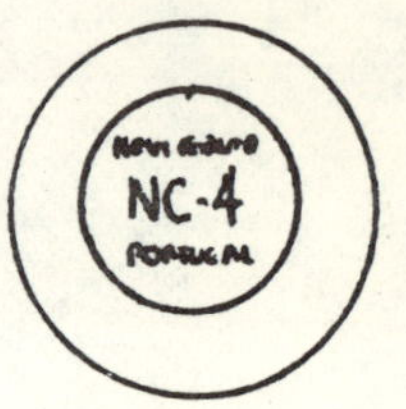

124. Good Conduct (Marine Corps) Old suspension
125. Good Conduct (Marine Corps) Present suspension

Awarded for: Good conduct for three-year periods of continuous active service.

Ribbon: Scarlet with navy blue center.

Notes: Bronze stars denote subsequent awards.

126. NC-4 Medal

Awarded for: The crew of the NC-4 flying boat who made the 1st transatlantic flight of 1919.

Ribbon: From left to right, red, white, blue, green, red.

127. Special Medal for Heroism

Awarded for: Presentated posthumously to four Army Chaplains who sacrificed their lives during WW II by giving their life jackets to fellow soldiers following the tarpedoing of their troopship, the Dorchester.

Ribbon: Colors unknown

Notes: The drawing shows the reverse of the medal. This medal is very rare, as only 12 were made.

128. Peary Polar Expedition Medal (1908–1909)

Awarded for: Members of the Expedition.

Ribbon: Ivory with two stripes of turquoise.

129. United States Antarctic Expedition Medal (1939–1941)

Awarded for: Members of the 1st U.S. expedition, it was lead by Admiral Byrd. (earlier explorations by Admiral Byrd had been privately financed.)

Ribbon: Ice blue on each side, with white center in which are two blue stripes.

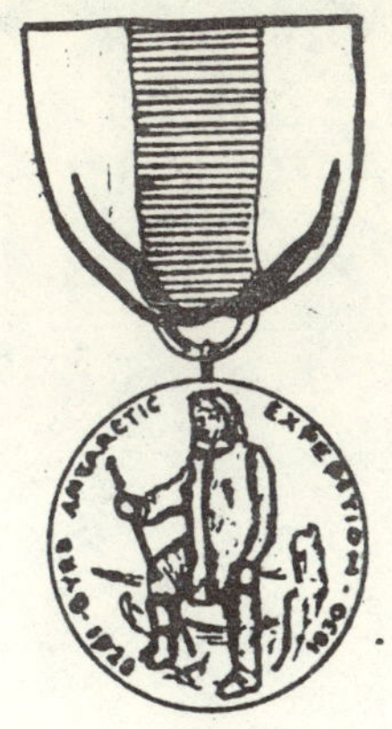

130. Second Byrd Antarctic Expedition Medal

Awarded for: Six months service at Little America or command of either expedition ship.

Ribbon: Plain white

131. Byrd Antarctic Expedition Medal (1st)

Awarded for: All members of the expedition. Made in gold for Adm. Byrd, silver for officers, bronze for all others.

Ribbon: White with blue center.

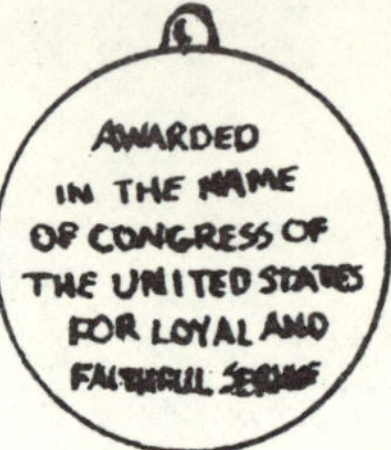

132. Selective Service Medal

Awarded for: Two years service in the Selective Service System (Draft Board

Ribbon: Orange-yellow divided by stripes of navy blue, the center stripe is also navy blue.

133.

134.

135.

136.

137.

138.

133. Armed Forces Reserve Medal (Marine Corps)
134. Armed Forces Reserve Medal (Air Force)
135. Armed Forces Reserve Medal (National Guard)
136. Armed Forces Reserve Medal Army & Organized Reserve
137. Armed Forces Reserve Medal (Navy)
138. Armed Forces Reserve Medal (Coast Guard)

Awarded for: Ten years of honorable service in reserve components of the Armed Forces

Ribbon: Same for all services, buff colored with three narrow blue stripes at edge and wide one in center.

Notes: Obverse of all the same, reverse as shown above.

139. Army Reserve Components Achievement Medal

Awarded for: Satisfactory service in an Army National Guard or Army Reserve troop program unit for a period of 4 years.

Ribbon: Red center flanked by white, blue and yellow edges.

140. Air Reserve Forces Meritorious Service Medal

Awarded for: Four continuous years of exemplary behavior, efficiency, and fidelity while serving in an enlisted status.

Ribbon: A.F. blue center, flanked each side by dark blue, yellow, dark blue, white, light blue edges.

141. Naval Reserve Meritorious Service Medal

Awarded for: Four years service in Naval Reserve after July 1, 1958.

Ribbon: Dark blue center stripe flanked by wide red stripes and then thin stripes of gold and then blue edges.

142. Organized Marine Corps Reserve Medal

Awarded for: Four years service (and 38 drills) with an organized unit of Marine Reserve.

Ribbon: Red center flanked by wide yellow, narrow blue, a white and a red at either edge.

Notes: A few of this medal can be found with the word "Fleet" before Marine Corps Reserve.

143. Naval Reserve Medal

Awarded for: Ten years service in Naval Reserve.

Ribbon: Red, with stripe of yellow, navy blue, another of yellow at each edge.

Notes: Obsolete 1958, Armed Forces Reserve Medal now awarded in its place.

144. National Defense Service Medal

Awarded for: Active service between June 27, 1950, and July 27, 1959

Ribbon: In the center a wide yellow stripe flanked by stripes of red, white, blue, white, and wide red stripes.

145. Victory Medal, World War II

Awarded for: Service in WW II.

Ribbon: Red center flanked each side by white, and then a rainbow pattern.

146. Victory Medal, World War I

Awarded for: Service in WW I

Ribbon: Red center flanked each side by a rainbow pattern.

147. **Andre Medal**

Awarded for: The capture of Major John Andre, a British intelligence officer. It was awarded to only three American militiamen. This medal was the 1st decoration created by Congress (1780).

Ribbon: Unknown.

147. NASA Distinguished Service Medal (Type 1)

Awarded for: Exceptionally meritorious service to NASA.

Ribbon: White center stripe flanked by light blue, medium blue, Navy blue at edges.

148. NASA Distinguished Service Medal (Type 2)

Awarded for: Exceptionally meritorious service to NASA.

Ribbon: Wide navy blue center flanked by light blue, medium blue at edges.

149. NASA Medal for Distinguished Public Service

Awarded for: Contributions to NASA mission.

Ribbon: Wide navy blue center flanked each side by light blue with gold center stripe.

150. NASA Medal for Exceptional Scientific Achievement

Awarded for: Scientific accomplishments

Ribbon: White center stripe flanked each side by dark blue, light blue, medium blue, edged in light blue.

151. NASA Medal for Exceptional Bravery

Awarded for: Exemplary and courageous handling of an emergency.

Ribbon: Center of red flanked by light blue, navy blue, light blue, and edged in medium blue.

152. NASA Exceptional Service Medal

Awarded for: Service or creative abilites.

Ribbon: Wide medium blue center edged with gold, black, gold.

153. NASA Outstanding Leadership Medal

Awarded for: Leadership

Ribbon: Medium blue center flanked each side by light blue, navy blue, light blue edged in medium blue.

154. Civilian Medal for Valor, Air Force

Awarded for: Competence or courage in any capacity of civilian employment.

Ribbon: Light blue with red center stripe flanked either side by yellow, blue yellow.

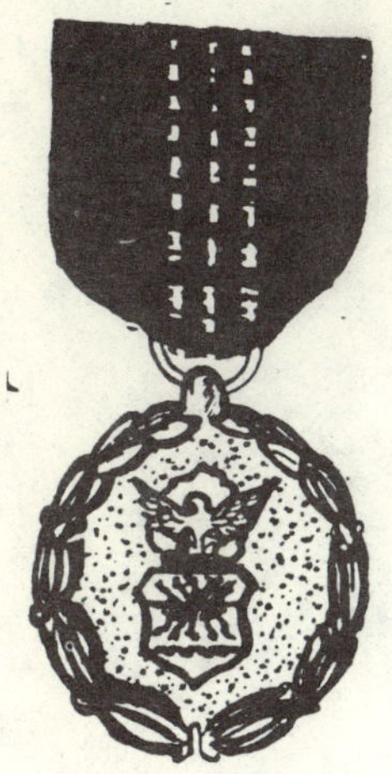

155. Exceptional Civilian Service Medal, Air Force

Awarded for: Exceptional service or acts of heroism involing risk of life.

Ribbon: Blue with broken orange stripes in center.

156. Distinguished Civilian Service Medal, U.S. Navy

Awarded for: Exceptionally meritorious service to the department, or acts of heroism involving risk of life.

Ribbon: Gold with three narrow stripes of blue.

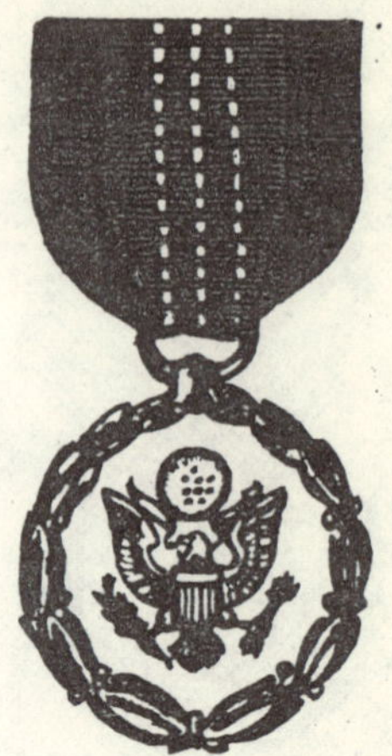

157. Navy Distinguished Public Service Award

Awarded for: Special contributions to the Department of Navy.

Ribbon: Navy blue and golden yellow.

158. Exceptional Civilian Service Award, Army

Awarded for: Exceptional service or acts of heroism involving risk of life.

Ribbon: Blue with broken white stripes in center.

Notes: Sometimes a cash award accompanies this medal.

159. Distinguished Civilian Service Medal, Army

Awarded for: Exceptional service

Ribbon: White, with separate stripes of blue, red, blue near each edge.

160. Outstanding Civilian Service Medal, Army

Awarded for: Exceptional service

Ribbon: White with six stripes of red, in center of each red stripe is very thin stripe of blue.

Notes: This medal is the same as number 159 except for the ribbon.

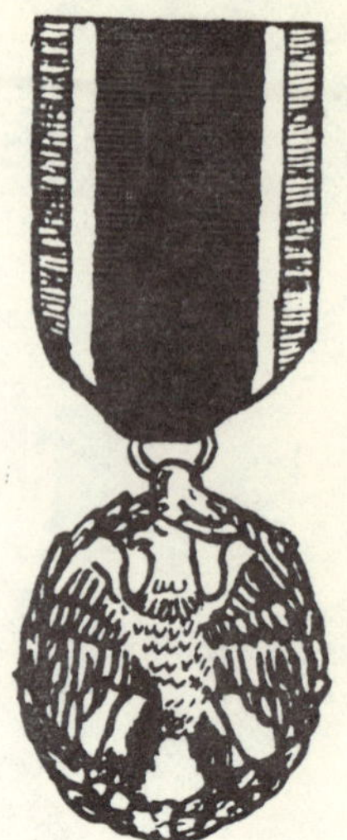

161. Achievement Medal, Coast Guard

Awarded for: Outstanding achievement.

Ribbon: White center stripe bordered by wide green stripe, wide orange stripe, green on either edge.

Notes: This medal is also known as Secretary of the Treasury Commendation and also as Secretary of Transportion Commendation.

162. Presidents Award for Distinguished Federal Civilian Service

Awarded for: Long and distinguished career or extraordinary achieve – ments.

Ribbon: Dark blue with white and blue on either edge.

163. National Security Medal

Awarded for: Valor or distinguished achievement in the field of intelligence. This medal is now obsolete, and very rare.

Ribbon: Dark blue with agold pattern in center.

164. National Security Agency Exceptional Service Medal

Awarded for: Exceptional service

Ribbon: Center is red, flanked each side by yellow wide band of green and edged in yellow.

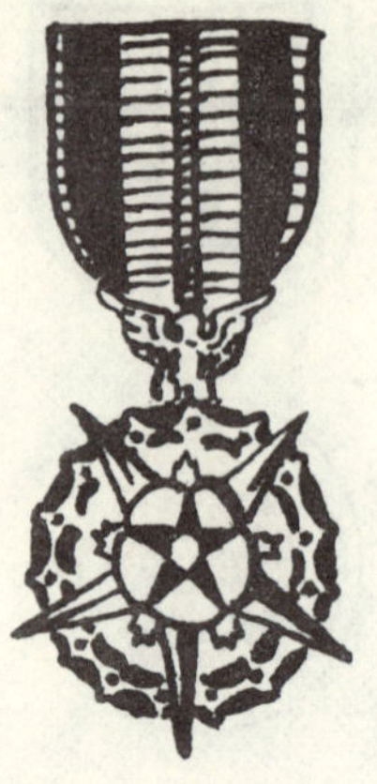

165. Congressional Space Medal of Honor

Awarded for: Meritorious contributions to the nation by any astronaut.

Ribbon: Center red flanked by white, , blue, dark blue, and gold at either edge.

Notes: This medal has a 1/4 carat diamond in center.

166. Secretary of Defense Distinguished Service Medal

Awarded for: Meritorious service

Ribbon: Center of red flanked by gold light blue edges.

167. Department of Defense Distinguished Public Service Award

Awarded for: Meritorious service

Ribbon: Blue with white at both edges and two white stripes near center.

168. Department of Defense Distinguished Civian Service Award

Awarded for: Distinguished service.

Ribbon: Blue with broken stripes of white.

169. Secretary of Defense Meritorious Civilian Service Award

Awarded for: Meritorious service to the Department.

Ribbon: Gold with three broken stripes of blue.

170. Defense Communications Agency Exceptional Civilian Award

Awa.ded for: Outstanding performance.

Ribbon: Dark blue with two gold stripes at center and at either edge.

171. U.S. Department of State Distinguished Honor Award

Awarded for: Outstanding Service to the department.

Ribbon: White, with three navy blue stripes.

Notes: The Department of State awards a Superior Honor and a Meritorious Honor Award and are the same as the above except for name on obverse and ribbon color plus each are made of different metals, Gold, Silver, Bronze.

172. Environmental Protection Agency Exceptional Service Medal

Awarded for: Outstanding Service and Leadership.

Ribbon: Green center flanked by white light green, white and blue edges.

Notes: This medal come in gold, silver, and bronze, ribbons on each are different.

173. Agency for International Development Distinguished Award

Awarded for: Outstanding Service

Ribbon: Light blue center flanked each side by dark blue,, white, dark blue, white, red edges.

Notes: This medals comes in gold, silver, and bronze

174. Vererans Administration Distinguished Career Award

Awarded for: Outstanding effciency and dedc ation and awarded at time of retirement.

Ribbon: Green

Notes: The Veterans Administration awards two other medals, Exceptional Service and Meritorious Service and are same as above except for name on obverse and ribbon color.

175. General Accounting Office Distinguished Service Award

Awarded for: Ten years of exceptional efficiency.

Ribbon: Navy blue center flanked on each side by green, white, green, red, gold, red, white, and blue edges.

176. Department of Transportation Achievement Award

Awarded for: Outstanding leadership.

Ribbon: Left to right, orange, black, white, black, orange, white, blue, white, orange, black, white, black, orange.

Notes: This Dept. awards three others, Meritorious Achievement, Award for Valor, and Award for Superior Achievement and all are same in design.

177. U.S. Information Agency Distinguished Honor

Awarded for: Exceptional service in national or international matters.

Ribbon: Navy blue

Notes: This award has three grades, Distinguished, Superior, and Meritorious (name of each on reverse)

178. Dept. of Defense, Civil Preparedness Agency Distinguished Civilian Service

Awarded for: Service or acts of importance to the agency

Ribbon: Light blue center flanked each side by dark blue, yellow, light blue and yellow on each edge.

179. Defense Intelligence Agency Exceptional Civilian Service

Awarded for: Notable performance or act of significance.

Ribbon: Light blue center flanked by navy blue, gold and again light blue.

180. Defense Intelligence Agency Meritorious Civilian Service

Awarded for: Service and meritorious performance.

Ribbon: Light blue center flanked each side by gold, navy blue edges.

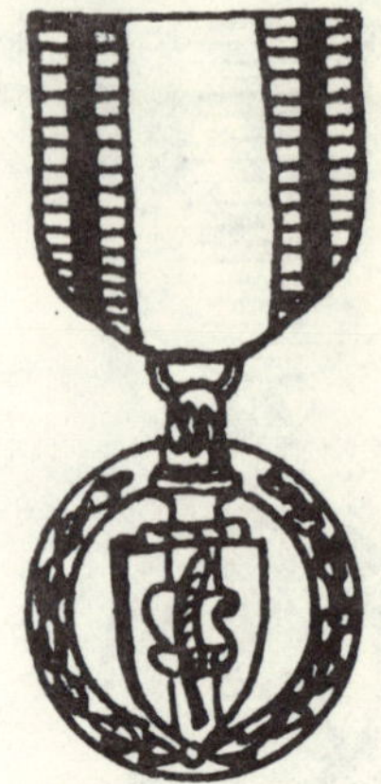

181. U.S. Public Health Service Commendation

Awarded for: Proficiency or dedication, high performance, or unique skills.

Ribbon: Center purple, flanked each side by white with black edges.

Notes: This medal comes in three classes, gold, silver and bronze, Distinguished Service, Meritorious Service, and Commendation.

182. Defense Contract Audit Agency Distinguished Civilian Service

Awarded for: Exceptionally meritorious service to the Agency.

Ribbon: Center yellow, flanked each side by white, turquoise, black, turquoise.

Notes: This medal comes in gold for Distinguished, and silver for Meritorious awards.